Contents

Who was Leonardo da Vinci?   4

Early years   6

Life in Florence   8

Becoming a master   10

On his own   12

On to Milan   14

Special skills   16

The Last Supper   18

Florence   20

New ideas   22

The secret smile   24

With King and Pope   26

Last years in France   28

Timeline   30

Glossary   31

More books to read and paintings to see   31

Index   32

Who was Leonardo da Vinci?

Leonardo da Vinci was a great painter who lived in Italy 500 years ago. Leonardo lived at a time when art was becoming important.

The Life and Work of...

Leonardo da Vinci

Sean Connolly

First published in Great Britain by
Heinemann Library,
Halley Court, Jordan Hill, Oxford OX2 8EJ
a division of Reed Educational and Professional
Publishing Ltd.
Heinemann is a registered trademark of Reed
Educational & Professional Publishing Ltd.

OXFORD   MELBOURNE   AUCKLAND
JOHANNESBURG BLANTYRE GABORONE
IBADAN PORTSMOUTH (NH) USA CHICAGO

Designed byCelia Floyd
Illustrations by Sally Barton
Originated by Dot Gradations
Printed in Hong Kong/China

04 03 02 01 00
10 9 8 7 6 5 4 3 2 1

ISBN 0 431 09188 9
This title is also available in a hardback library
edition (ISBN 0 431 09180 3).

British Library Cataloguing in Publication Data

Connolly, Sean
  Life and work of Leonardo Da Vinci
  1. Leonardo, da Vinci, 1452-1519 – Juvenile literature
  2. Painters – Italy – Biography – Juvenile literature
  3. Painting, Renaissance – Italy – Juvenile literature
  I. Title
  759.5

Acknowledgements
The Publishers would like to thank the following for
permission to reproduce photographs:

Pages 5, 19, Leonardo da Vinci 'The Last Supper',
Credit: Giraudon. Page 7, Leonardo da Vinci 'The
Annunciation', Credit: Giraudon. Page 8, Florence,
Tuscany, Italy, Credit: Colorific! Page 9, Leonardo
da Vinci 'The Baptism of Christ', Credit: Giraudon.
Page 11, Leonardo da Vinci 'Ginevra de' Benci',
Credit: National Gallery of Art, Washington. Page
13, Leonardo da Vinci 'The Adoration of the Magi',
Credit: Giraudon. Page 15, Leonardo da Vinci 'The
Virgin of the Rocks', Credit: Giraudon. Page 16,
Leonardo da Vinci 'Design for a helicopter', Credit:
AKG. Page 17, Leonardo da Vinci 'Sketch for the
proposed 'Tiburio' of Milan cathedral', Credit:
Biblioteca Trivulziana. Page 21, Leonardo da Vinci
'Cartoon for the Virgin and child with Saint Anne',
Credit: Giraudon. Page 22, Leonardo da Vinci
'Design for assault vehicles', Credit: AKG. Page 23,
Leonardo da Vinci 'Sketch to show a technique of
pushing down the walls', Credit: AKG. Page 25,
Leonardo da Vinci 'Mona Lisa', Credit: Giraudon.
Page 26, Leonardo da Vinci 'Studies for a Nativity',
Credit: SCALA. Page 27, Leonardo da Vinci 'Saint
John the Baptist', Credit: Giraudon. Page 28,
Chateau Clos Lucé, Credit: Pix. Page 29, Leonardo
da Vinci 'Self-Portrait', Credit: Image Select.

Cover photograph reproduced with permission of
Bridgeman Art Library

Our thanks to Paul Flux for his comments in the
preparation of this book.

Every effort has been made to contact copyright
holders of any material reproduced in this book.
Any omissions will be rectified in subsequent
printings if notice is given to the Publisher.

For more information about Heinemann Library
books, or to order, please telephone
+44(0)1865 888066, or send a fax to +441865 314091.
You can visit our web site at www.heinemann.co.uk

Any words appearing in the text in bold, **like this**,
are explained in the Glossary.

Leonardo was also a **sculptor**, a poet and an **inventor**. He loved nature and science. This helped him make his pictures look like real life.

Early years

Leonardo was born on 15 April 1452 in Vinci, Italy. The name 'da Vinci' means 'from Vinci'. When he was young, Leonardo's uncle Francesco taught him about the countryside.

Leonardo never forgot the long walks in the hills with his uncle. Many years later he could still paint all the plants he had seen.

Life in Florence

In 1470 Leonardo went to live in a city called Florence. He learned to paint in the **studio** of Andrea del Verrocchio. Andrea was one of many great painters in Florence.

Two years later Leonardo painted the angel on the left in this painting by Andrea. Andrea thought the angel was the best part of the painting.

Becoming a master

Leonardo finished his **studies** soon after painting the angel. He could have set up his own **studio**. Instead he stayed in Andrea's house.

In 1474 he painted this **portrait** of a young woman. The dark trees behind her face make her skin look bright.

On his own

Leonardo was 25 years old when he began working for himself. He had learned a lot from Andrea. He had also met many important people.

This unfinished early painting tells us how
Leonardo worked. The colours are all shades
of brown. Leonardo would add the brighter
colours later.

On to Milan

In 1482 Leonardo went to work for the ruler of the city of Milan. Leonardo lived there with a family of artists called Preda.

Leonardo and the Preda family worked on this painting of Mary with the infant Jesus. The lovely mixture of light and dark was the work of Leonardo.

Special skills

Leonardo **studied** different subjects in Milan. He was very interested in the human body and how water moved. Leonardo also **designed** many things like this helicopter.

You can still see many of Leonardo's designs. This sketch shows how Leonardo planned to make the **dome** of the great **cathedral** in Milan better.

The Last Supper

In 1495 Leonardo began a huge **mural** of Christ's Last Supper. The picture shows how he wanted to paint what people are thinking as well as how they look.

The Last Supper shows Christ and his 12 **apostles**. Leonardo's picture looks like a real supper. It shows all of the men busy talking and listening.

Florence

In 1499 Milan was attacked. Leonardo escaped and went back to Florence. There he met many other artists.

Other artists liked Leonardo's work. He could show gentle movements and even feelings in his pictures. This **cartoon** shows the Virgin Mary with Jesus and her mother.

New ideas

Leonardo soon had a chance to show his other skills. In 1502 he became the main **military engineer** in Central Italy.

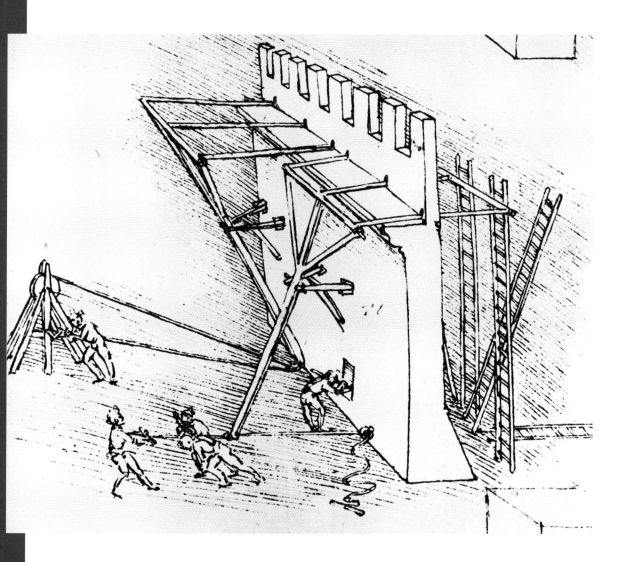

Leonardo drew plans for weapons, **fortresses** and bridges. This sketch of putting up a fortress wall is from a book of his drawings called *Codex Atlanticus*.

The secret smile

Leonardo was very busy but he still found time to work on a special **portrait**. The result was the *Mona Lisa*, one of the most famous paintings in the world.

No one can be sure who this woman really was.
Her smile has fascinated people for many years.
She looks like she is keeping a secret.

With King and Pope

In 1507 Leonardo became court painter to a French King who was living in Milan. Seven years later Leonardo moved to Rome as a guest of the **Pope**. This is a sketch he made in 1482 for a painting called *Adoration of the Kings*.

Leonardo's last pictures were **religious**. The hand of Saint John the Baptist seems to come right out of this painting.

Last years in France

Leonardo lived as the guest of another French King for his last three years. He made many drawings in his large house in France. He died on 2 May 1519, aged 67.

This **self-portrait** shows Leonardo as an old man. He has lost his teeth and much of his hair. His eyes are still strong.

Timeline

1452   Leonardo da Vinci born in Vinci, central Italy on 15 April.

1470   Leonardo moves to Florence and begins training with Andrea del Verrocchio.

1474   The first printed book in English is made.

1477   Leonardo leaves Andrea's **studio** to work on his own.

1482   Leonardo moves to Milan.

1492   Christopher Columbus discovers the West Indies.

1495   Leonardo begins *The Last Supper*.

1499   Leonardo returns to Florence.

1502   Leonardo becomes **military engineer** in central Italy.

1505-15 Leonardo paints the *Mona Lisa*.

1507   Leonardo moves to Milan as a guest of King Louis XII of France.

1509   Henry VIII becomes King of England.

1514-16 Leonardo lives in Rome as guest of the **Pope**.

1516   Leonardo moves to France as guest of King François I.

1519   Leonardo dies at Chateau Clos-Lucé, France on 2 May.

Glossary

apostle one of the 12 close friends and followers of Jesus Christ

cartoon quick drawing done before making a painting

cathedral large church, usually in a city

design to think of an idea or plan and put it on paper

dome rounded roof

fortress strong building to guard against enemies

inventor someone who thinks of new ideas for doing or making things

military engineer someone who plans and makes weapons and fortresses

mural picture painted on to a wall

Pope the leader of the Roman Catholic Church

portrait painting of a person

religious to do with what people believe in

sculptor someone who carves wood or stone to make works of art

self-portrait picture that an artist paints of himself or herself

studio building or room where an artist works

study learn about a subject

More books to read

What Makes a Leonardo a Leonardo?, Richard Muhlberger. New York Metropolitan Museum of Art/Cherrytree Books

Famous Lives: Artists, Jillian Powell, Wayland Publishers

More paintings to see

Panels for an Ancona, Leonardo da Vinci, National Gallery, London

The Virgin of the rocks, Leonardo da Vinci, National Gallery, London

Burlington House Cartoon (Virgin and child with St Anne), Leonardo da Vinci, National Gallery, London

31

Index

birth   6

Codex Atlanticus   23

death   28

Florence   8, 20

France   28

Italy   4, 5, 8, 14, 16, 17, 20, 22, 26

Last Supper   5, 18, 19

Milan   14, 16, 17, 20, 26

Mona Lisa   24, 25

Preda family   14, 15

Verrocchio, Andrea del   8, 9, 10, 12

Vinci   6